This Coloring Book Belongs To:

Valentine's Day Coloring Book For Toddlers © 2019 by Mango Tree Publishing
All rights reserved. No part of this book may be used or reproduced in any manner whatsoever without written permission except in the case of brief quotations embodied in critical articles and reviews.
First Edition: 2019

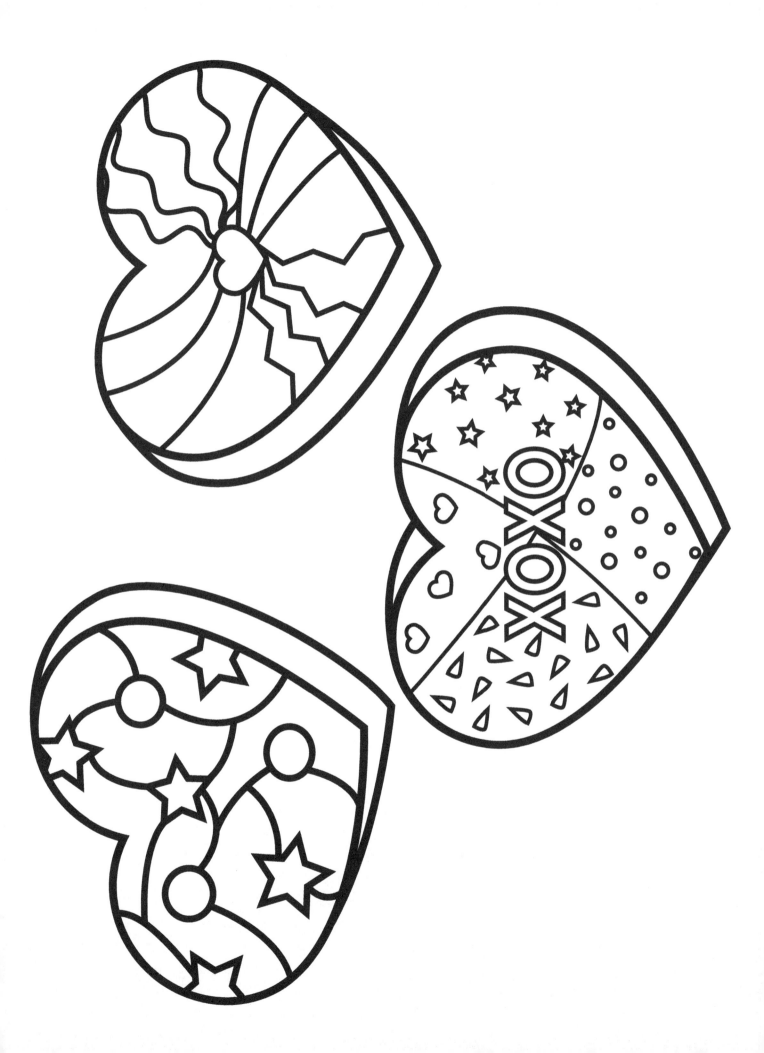

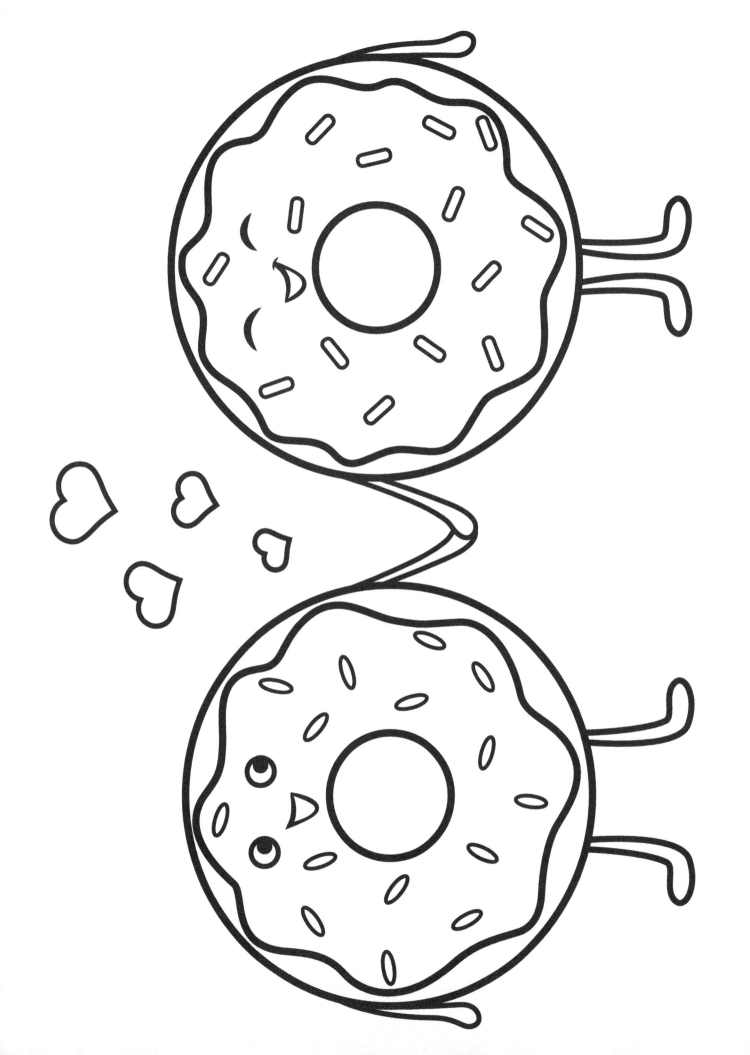

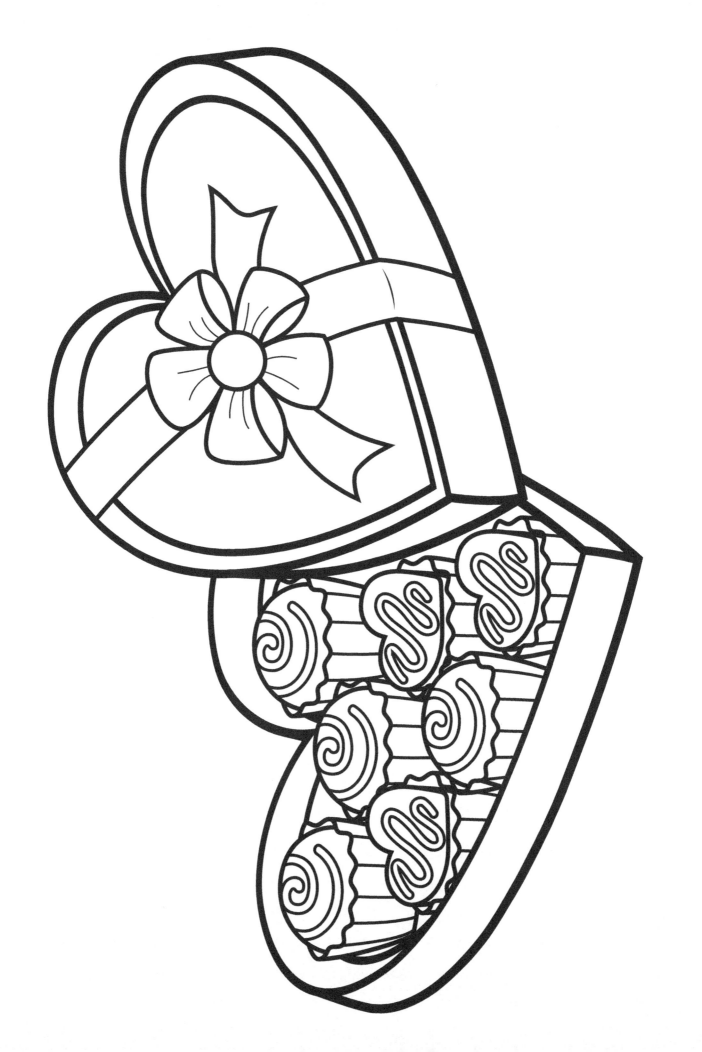

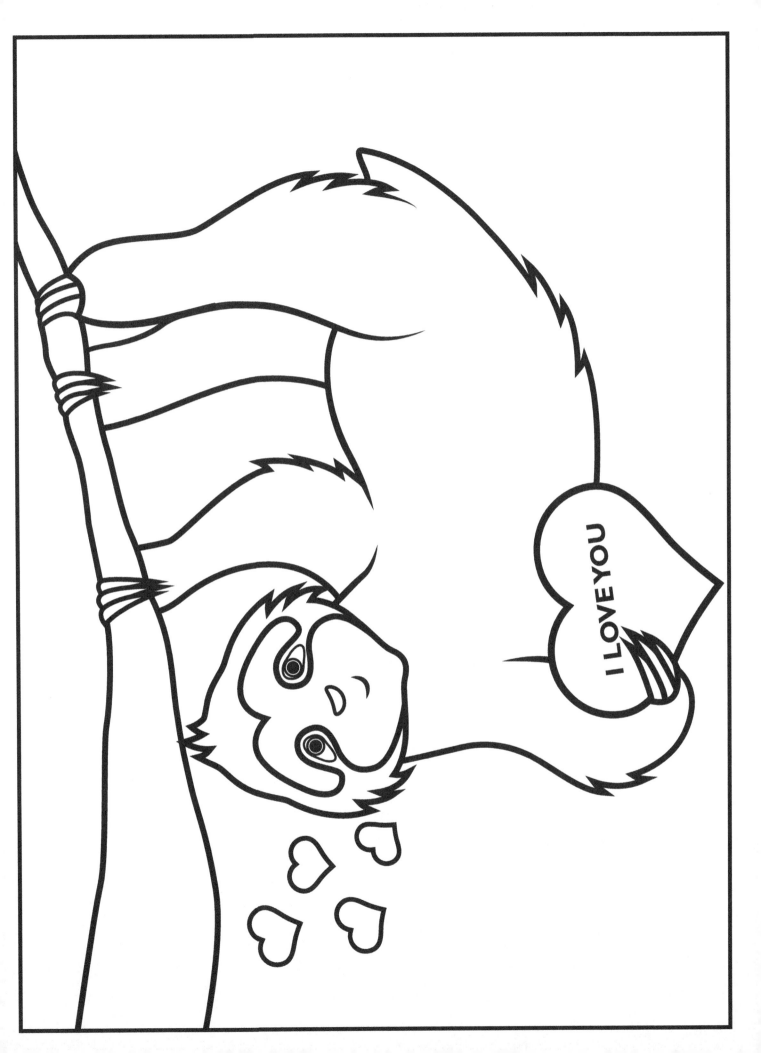

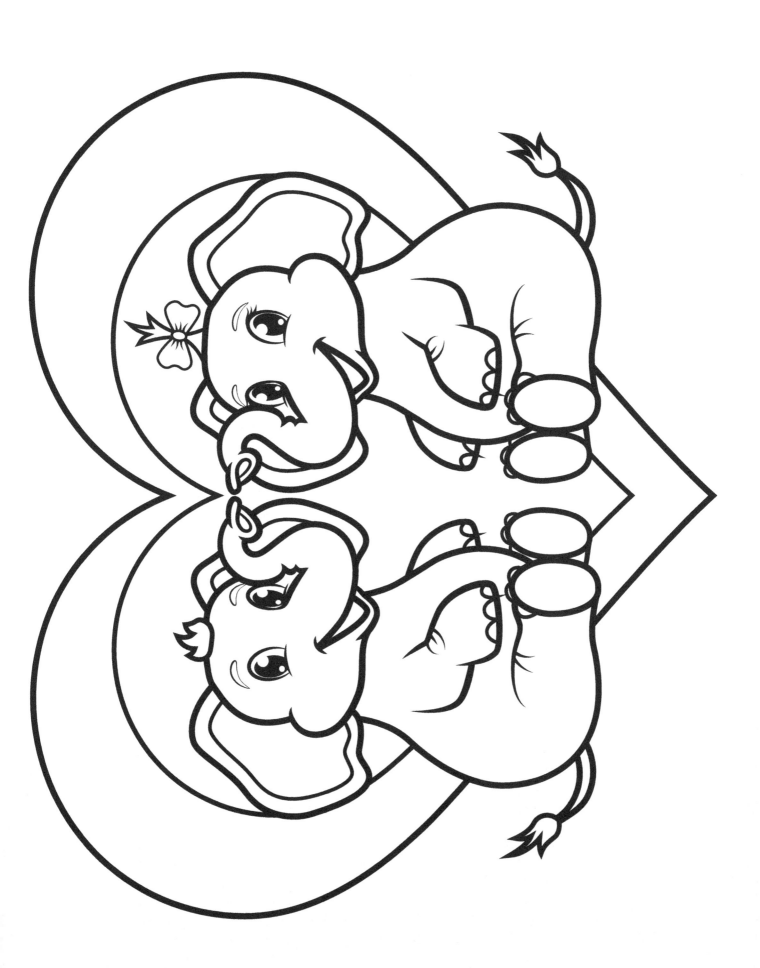

Made in the USA
Las Vegas, NV
07 February 2024